HISTORY'S MOST INFLUENTIAL

INVENTORS

FROM THE Paleolithic Period TO THE Early 1800s

Cro-Magnons to Robert Fulton

EDITED BY ROBERT CURLEY

Britannica Educational Publishing

IN ASSOCIATION WITH

ROSEN

EDUCATIONAL SERVICES

Published in 2025 by Britannica Educational Publishing
(a trademark of Encyclopædia Britannica, Inc.)
in association with Rosen Educational Services, LLC
2544 Clinton Street, Buffalo, NY 14224.

Distributed exclusively by Rosen Educational Services.
For a listing of additional Britannica Educational Publishing titles, call toll free (800) 237-9932.

First Edition

Britannica Educational Publishing
Michael I. Levy: Executive Editor
Marilyn L. Barton: Senior Coordinator, Production Control
Steven Bosco: Director, Editorial Technologies
Lisa S. Braucher: Senior Producer and Data Editor
Yvette Charboneau: Senior Copy Editor
Kathy Nakamura: Manager, Media Acquisition
Robert Curley: Manager, Science and Technology

Editor: Greg Roza
Book design: Michael Flynn

Photo credits: Cover, p. 43 https://commons.wikimedia.org/wiki/File:Watt_James_von_Breda.jpg; p. 6 Jakub Korczyk/Shutterstock.com; p. 11 Ntguilty/Shutterstock.com; p. 16 Javier Jaime/Shutterstock.com; pp. 19, 37 Everett Collection/Shutterstock.com; p. 23 https://commons.wikimedia.org/wiki/File:Christiaan_Huygens-painting.jpeg; p. 28 https://commons.wikimedia.org/wiki/File:Anthonie_van_Leeuwenhoek_(1632-1723)._Natuurkundige_te_Delft_Rijksmuseum_SK-A-957.jpeg.

Cataloging-in-Publication Data

Names: Curley, Robert, 1955-.
Title: From the Paleolithic Period to the early 1800s: Cro-Magnons to Robert Fulton / edited by Robert Curley.
Description: New York : Britannica Educational Publishing, in Association with Rosen Educational Services, 2025. | Series: History's most influential inventors | Includes glossary and index.
Identifiers: ISBN 9781641900874 (library bound) | ISBN 9781641900867 (pbk) | ISBN 9781641900881 (ebook)
Subjects: LCSH: Inventors--Biography. | Inventions--History.
Classification: LCC T39.F766 2025 | DDC 609.2'2--dc23

Manufactured in the United States of America

CPSIA Compliance Information: Batch #CSBRIT25. For further information contact Rosen Publishing at 1-800-237-9932.

CONTENTS

INTRODUCTION

As we enjoy great advantages from the inventions of others, we should be glad of an opportunity to serve others by any invention of ours; and this we should do freely and generously.
—Benjamin Franklin (1706–1790)

Life has been transformed over the years through the efforts of the men and women who had the brilliance, diligence, and creativity to come up with new and better ways of doing things. This book focuses on the inventions of people living between the Paleolithic period and the early 1800s. As detailed throughout these pages, their inventions spawned many more inventions, speeding up the pace of progress even further.

Although many of these inventions have been around for millennia, they are still important today. For example, Cro-Magnon stone tools were a world-changing technological feat. The Archimedes screw water pump, invented in the 3rd century BCE, is still in use today. And recorded history would not have been possible without Cai Lun's invention of paper in 105 CE.

The old saying, "Necessity is the mother of invention," couldn't be more true. Inventors have had a knack for recognizing a need or problem in society and then discovering a way to fill that need or solve that problem. For example, in the 15th century, as the number of universities in Europe grew and public literacy spread, a more efficient method was needed for reproducing books—a demand that was met by Johannes Gutenberg's printing press.

Sometimes it was the inventor's own necessity that gave birth to invention. Frustrated at having to change pairs of glasses whenever he switched from reading to viewing objects at a distance, Benjamin Franklin invented a new type of glasses—bifocals—that could easily accommodate both views.

Intelligence and curiosity are unquestionably important assets for inventors. What ultimately fueled the spark of discovery and led inventors to their "eureka" moment was unique to each person. Some inventions throughout history have occurred purely by accident. For other inventions, however, the process was painstakingly slow and required many hours of trial and error.

The creations of the influential figures profiled in this book have improved life by keeping people healthier, helping them to communicate and work more efficiently, and allowing them to travel farther. Antonie van Leeweunhoek's forays into bacteriology, James Watt's steam engine, and John Loudon McAdam's road system are just a few examples of such inventions and their far-reaching effects.

So many inventors have made important contributions that to mention them all here would far exceed the space limitations of this book. The figures who have been included are among the greatest and most prolific inventors of all time. They were selected because their inventions have altered the course of people's lives and have left an indelible stamp on human history.

CRO-MAGNON

Cro-Magnon was a population of early *Homo sapiens* dating from the Upper Paleolithic Period (*c.* 40,000 to *c.* 10,000 years ago) in Europe. In their ancient cave habitations they left behind traces of ingenious stone tools, carved statuettes and figurines, and painted scenes of striking beauty that are considered to be among the greatest treasures of human creativity.

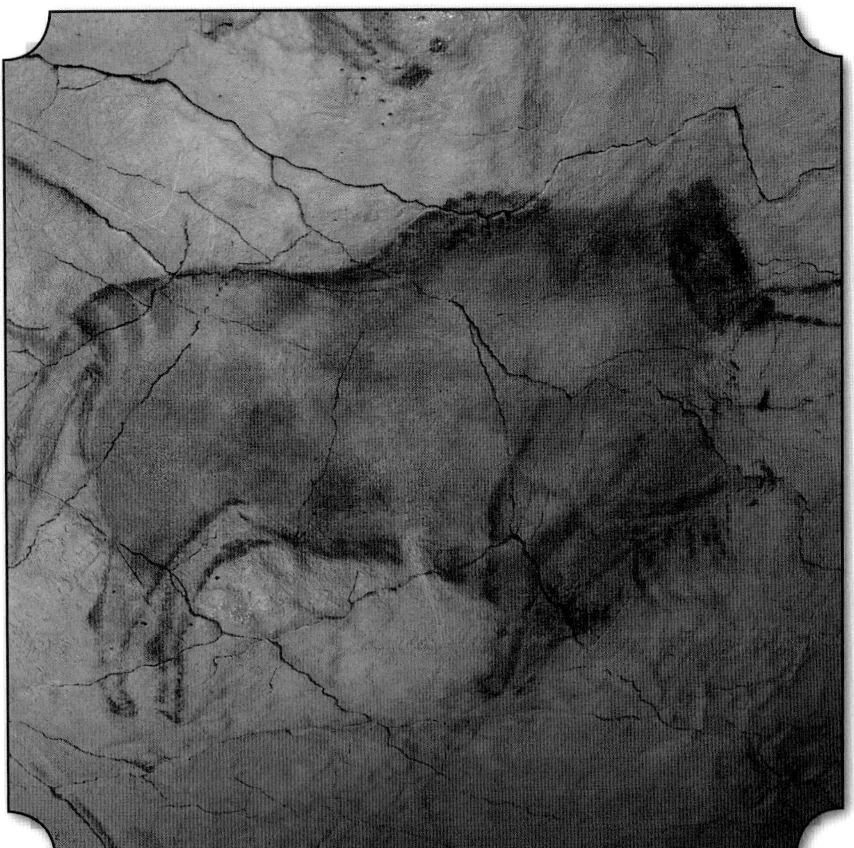

The Altamira cave in Spain features images of bison and other animals. It is an exceptional example of Paleolithic cave art.

In 1868, in a shallow cave near the town of Les Eyzies-de-Tayac in the Dordogne region of southwestern France, a number of obviously ancient human skeletons were found. The cave was investigated by the French geologist Édouard Lartet, who uncovered five archaeological layers. The human bones found in the topmost layer proved to be between 10,000 and 35,000 years old. The prehistoric humans revealed by this find were called Cro-Magnon and have since been considered, along with Neanderthals (*H. neanderthalensis*), to be representative of prehistoric humans.

Cro-Magnons were robustly built and powerful and are presumed to have been about 5 feet 5 inches to 5 feet 7 inches (about 166 to 171 cm) tall. The body was generally heavy and solid, apparently with strong musculature. The forehead was straight, with slight browridges, and the face short and wide. Cro-Magnons were the first humans (genus *Homo*) to have a prominent chin. The brain capacity was about 100 cubic inches (1,600 cc), somewhat larger than the average for modern humans. It is thought that Cro-Magnons were probably fairly tall compared with other early human species.

It is still hard to say precisely where Cro-Magnons belong in recent human evolution, but they had a culture that produced a variety of sophisticated tools such as retouched blades, end scrapers, "nosed" scrapers, the chisel-like tool known as a burin, and fine bone tools. They also seem to have made tools for smoothing and scraping leather. Some Cro-Magnons have been associated with the Gravettian industry, or Upper Perigordian industry, which is characterized by an abrupt retouching technique that produces tools with flat backs. Cro-Magnon dwellings are most often found in deep caves and in shallow caves formed by rock overhangs, although primitive huts, either lean-tos against rock walls or those built completely from stones, have been found. The rock shelters were used year-round; the Cro-Magnons seem to have been a settled people, moving only when necessary to find new hunting or because of environmental changes.

Like the Neanderthals, the Cro-Magnon people buried their dead. The first examples of art by prehistoric peoples are Cro-Magnon. The Cro-Magnons carved and sculpted small engravings, reliefs, and statuettes not only of humans but also of animals. Their human figures generally depict large-breasted, wide-hipped, and often obviously pregnant women, from which it is assumed that these figures had significance in fertility rites. Numerous depictions of animals are found in Cro-Magnon cave paintings throughout France and Spain at sites such as Lascaux, Les Eyzies-de-Tayac, and Altamira, and some of them are surpassingly beautiful. It is thought that these paintings had some magic or ritual importance to the people. From the high quality of their art, it is clear that Cro-Magnons were not primitive amateurs but had previously experimented with artistic mediums and forms. Decorated tools and weapons show that they appreciated art for aesthetic purposes as well as for religious reasons.

It is difficult to determine how long the Cro-Magnons lasted and what happened to them. Presumably they were gradually absorbed into the European populations that came later. Individuals with some Cro-Magnon characteristics, commonly called Cro-Magnoids, have been found in the Mesolithic Period (8000 to 5000 BCE) and the Neolithic Period (5000 to 2000 BCE).

IMHOTEP

(b. 27th century BCE, Memphis, Egypt)

Imhotep (Greek: Imouthes) was a vizier, sage, architect, astrologer, and chief minister to Djoser (reigned 2630–2611 BCE), the second king of Egypt's third dynasty, who was later worshipped as the god of medicine in Egypt and in Greece, where he was identified with the Greek god of medicine, Asclepius. He is considered to have been the architect of the step pyramid built at the necropolis of Saqqārah in the city of Memphis. The oldest extant monument of hewn stone known to the world, the pyramid consists of six steps and attains a height of 200 feet (61 m).

Although no contemporary account has been found that refers to Imhotep as a practicing physician, ancient documents illustrating Egyptian society and medicine during the Old Kingdom (*c.* 2575– *c.* 2130 BCE) show that the chief magician of the pharaoh's court also frequently served as the nation's chief physician. Imhotep's reputation as the reigning genius of the time, his position in the court, his training as a scribe, and his becoming known as a medical demigod only 100 years after his death are strong indications that he must have been a physician of considerable skill.

Not until the Persian conquest of Egypt in 525 BCE was Imhotep elevated to the position of a full deity, replacing Nefertem in the great triad of Memphis, shared with his mythological parents Ptah, the creator of the universe, and Sekhmet, the goddess of war and pestilence. Imhotep's cult reached its zenith during Greco-Roman times, when his temples in Memphis and on the island of Philae (Arabic: *Jazīrat Fīlah*) in the Nile River were often crowded with sufferers who prayed and slept there with the conviction that the god would reveal remedies to them in their dreams. The only Egyptian mortal besides the 18th-dynasty sage and minister Amenhotep to attain the honor of total deification, Imhotep is still held in esteem by physicians who, like the eminent 19th-century British practitioner Sir William Osler, consider him "the first figure of a physician to stand out clearly from the mists of antiquity."

ARCHIMEDES

(b. *c.* 290–280 BCE, Syracuse, Sicily [now in Italy]—d. 212/211 BCE, Syracuse)

The most famous mathematician of ancient Greece, Archimedes is especially important for his discovery of the relation between the surface and volume of a sphere and its circumscribing cylinder and for his formulation of a hydrostatic principle (known as Archimedes' principle). As an inventor he is known for various ingenious (and perhaps mythical) optical and mechanical devices, including a device for raising water, still used in developing countries, known as the Archimedes screw.

Archimedes probably spent some time in Egypt early in his career, but he resided for most of his life in Syracuse, the principal Greek city-state in Sicily, where he was on intimate terms with its king, Hieron II. Archimedes published his works in the form of correspondence with the principal mathematicians of his time, including the Alexandrian scholars Conon of Samos and Eratosthenes of Cyrene. He played an important role in the defense of Syracuse against the siege laid by the Romans in 213 BCE by constructing war machines so effective that they long delayed the capture of the city. When Syracuse eventually fell to the Roman general Marcus Claudius Marcellus in the autumn of 212 or spring of 211 BCE, Archimedes was killed in the sack of the city.

Many of Archimedes's inventions are still used today.

Far more details survive about the life of Archimedes than about any other ancient scientist, but they are largely anecdotal, reflecting the impression that his mechanical genius made on the popular imagination. Thus, he is credited with inventing the Archimedes screw, and he is supposed to have made two "spheres" that Marcellus took back to Rome—one a star globe and the other a device (the details of which are uncertain) for mechanically representing the motions of the sun, the moon, and the planets. The story that he determined the proportion of gold and silver in a wreath made for Hieron by weighing it in water is probably true, but the version that has him leaping from the bath in which he supposedly got the idea and running naked through the streets shouting "Heurēka!" ("I have found it!") is popular embellishment. Equally apocryphal are the stories that he used a huge array of mirrors to burn the Roman ships besieging Syracuse; that he said, "Give me a place to stand and I will move the Earth"; and that a Roman soldier killed him because he refused to leave his mathematical diagrams—although all are popular reflections of his real interest in catoptrics (the branch of optics dealing with the reflection of light from mirrors, plane or curved), mechanics, and pure mathematics.

According to Plutarch (*c.* 46–119 CE), Archimedes had so low an opinion of the kind of practical invention at which he excelled and to which he owed his contemporary fame that he left no written work on such subjects. While it is true that most of his known works were of a theoretical character, his interest in mechanics nevertheless deeply influenced his mathematical thinking. Not only did he write works on the topics of theoretical mechanics and hydrostatics, but his treatise *Method Concerning Mechanical Theorems* shows that he used mechanical reasoning as a heuristic device for the discovery of new mathematical theorems.

CAI LUN

(b. 62? CE, Guiyang [now Leiyang, in present-day Hunan province], China—d. 121, China)

Cai Lun (courtesy name [zi] Jingzhong) was a Chinese court official who is traditionally credited with the invention of paper.

Cai Lun was a eunuch who entered the service of the imperial palace in 75 CE and was made chief eunuch under the emperor Hedi (reigned 88–105/106) of the Dong (Eastern) Han dynasty in the year 89. About the year 105 Cai conceived the idea of forming sheets of paper from the macerated bark of trees, hemp waste, old rags, and fishnets. The paper thus obtained was found to be superior in writing quality to cloth made of pure silk (the principal writing surface of the time), as well as being much less expensive to produce and having more abundant sources.

Cai reported his discovery to the emperor, who commended him for it. Important improvements were subsequently made to Cai's papermaking process by his apprentice, Zuo Bo, and the process was rapidly adopted throughout China, from which it eventually spread to the rest of the world. Cai himself was named a marquess in 114.

HERON OF ALEXANDRIA

(fl. *c.* 62 CE, Alexandria, Egypt)

Heron (or Hero) of Alexandria was a Greek geometer and inventor whose writings preserved for posterity a knowledge of the mathematics and engineering of Babylonia, ancient Egypt, and the Greco-Roman world.

Heron's most important geometric work, *Metrica*, was lost until 1896. It is a compendium, in three books, of geometric rules and formulas that Heron gathered from a variety of sources, some of them going back to ancient

Babylon, on areas and volumes of plane and solid figures. Book I enumerates means of finding the area of various plane figures and the surface areas of common solids. Included is a derivation of Heron's formula (actually, Archimedes' formula) for the area A of a triangle,

$$A = \sqrt{(s(s-a)(s-b)(s-c))}$$

in which a, b, and c are the lengths of the sides of the triangle, and s is one-half the triangle's perimeter. Book I also contains an iterative method known by the Babylonians (*c.* 2000 BCE) for approximating the square root of a number to arbitrary accuracy. (A variation on such an iterative method is frequently employed by computers today.) Book II gives methods for computing volumes of various solids, including the five regular Platonic solids. Book III treats the division of various plane and solid figures into parts according to some given ratio.

Other works on geometry ascribed to Heron are *Geometrica*, *Stereometrica*, *Mensurae*, *Geodaesia*, *Definitiones*, and *Liber Geëponicus*, which contain problems similar to those in the *Metrica*. However, the first three are certainly not by Heron in their present form, and the sixth consists largely of extracts from the first. Akin to these works is the *Dioptra*, a book on land surveying; it contains a description of the diopter, a surveying instrument used for the same purposes as the modern theodolite. The treatise also contains applications of the diopter to measuring celestial distances and describes a method for finding the distance between Alexandria and Rome from the difference between local times at which a lunar eclipse would be observed at the two cities. It ends with the description of an odometer for measuring the distance a wagon or cart travels. *Catoptrica* ("Reflection") exists only as a Latin translation of a work formerly thought to be a fragment of Ptolemy's *Optica*. In *Catoptrica* Heron explains the rectilinear propagation of light and the law of reflection.

Of Heron's writings on mechanics, all that remain in Greek are *Pneumatica*, *Automatopoietica*, *Belopoeica*, and *Cheirobalistra*. The *Pneumatica*, in two books, describes a menagerie of mechanical devices, or "toys": singing birds, puppets, coin-operated machines, a fire engine, a water organ, and his most famous invention, the aeolipile, the first steam-powered engine. This last device consisted of a hollow sphere mounted so that it could turn on a pair of hollow tubes that provided steam to the sphere from a cauldron. The steam escaped from the sphere from one or more bent tubes projecting from its equator, causing the sphere to revolve. The aeolipile is the first known device to transform steam into rotary motion. Like many other machines of the time that demonstrated basic mechanical principles, it was simply regarded as a curiosity or a toy and was not used for any practical purpose.

The *Belopoeica* ("Engines of War") purports to be based on a work by Ctesibius of Alexandria (fl. *c.* 270 BCE). Heron's *Mechanica*, in three books, survives only in an Arabic translation, somewhat altered. This work is cited by Pappus of Alexandria (fl. 300 CE), as is also the *Baroulcus* ("Methods of Lifting Heavy Weights"). *Mechanica*, which is closely based on the work of Archimedes, presents a wide range of engineering principles, including a theory of motion, a theory of the balance, methods of lifting and transporting heavy objects with mechanical devices, and how to calculate the center of gravity for various simple shapes. Both *Belopoeica* and *Mechanica* contain Heron's solution of the problem of two mean proportionals—two quantities, x and y, that satisfy the ratios $a:x = x:y = y:b$, in which a and b are known—which can be used to solve the problem of constructing a cube with double the volume of a given cube.

Applying heat to an aeolipile generates steam inside the water-filled sphere. As the steam escapes, the sphere revolves.

Only fragments of other treatises by Heron remain. One on water clocks is referred to by Pappus and the philosopher Proclus (410–485 CE). Another, a commentary on Euclid's *Elements*, is often quoted in a surviving Arabic work by Abu'l-'Abbās al-Fadl ibn Hātim al-Nayrīzī (*c.* 865–922).

JOHANNES GUTENBERG

(b. 14th century, Mainz [now in Ger.]—d. probably Feb. 3, 1468, Mainz)

Johann Gensfleisch zur Laden zum Gutenberg was a German craftsman and inventor who originated a method of printing from movable type that was used without important change until the 20th century. The unique elements of his invention consisted of a mold, with punch-stamped matrices (metal prisms used to mold the face of the type) with which type could be cast precisely and in large quantities; a type-metal alloy; a new press, derived from those used in wine making, papermaking, and bookbinding; and an oil-based printing ink. None of these features existed in Chinese or Korean printing, or in the existing European technique of stamping letters on various surfaces, or in woodblock printing.

Life

Gutenberg was the son of a patrician of Mainz. What little information exists about him, other than that he had acquired skill in metalwork, comes from documents of financial transactions. Exiled from Mainz in the course of a bitter struggle between the guilds of that city and the patricians, Gutenberg moved to Strassburg (now Strasbourg, France) probably between 1428 and 1430. Records put his presence there from 1434 to 1444. He engaged in such crafts as gem cutting, and he also taught crafts to a number of pupils.

Some of his partners, who became aware that Gutenberg was engaged in work that he kept secret from them, insisted that, since they had advanced him considerable sums, they should become partners in these activities as well. Thus, in 1438 a five-year contract was drawn up between him and three other men: Hans Riffe, Andreas Dritzehn, and Andreas Heilmann. It contained a clause whereby in case of the death of one of the partners, his heirs were not to enter the company but were to be compensated financially.

Invention of the Press

When Andreas Dritzehn died at Christmas 1438, his heirs, trying to circumvent the terms of the contract, began a lawsuit against Gutenberg in which they demanded to be made partners. They lost the suit, but the trial revealed that Gutenberg was working on a new invention. Witnesses testified that a carpenter named Conrad Saspach had advanced sums to Andreas Dritzehn for the building of a wooden press, and Hans Dünne, a goldsmith, declared that he had sold to Gutenberg, as early as 1436, 100 guilders' worth of printing materials. Gutenberg, apparently well along the way to completing his invention, was anxious to keep secret the nature of the enterprise.

After March 12, 1444, Gutenberg's activities are undocumented for a number of years, but it is doubtful that he returned immediately to Mainz, for the quarrel between patricians and guilds had been renewed in that city. In October 1448, however, Gutenberg was back in Mainz to borrow more money, which he received from a relative. By 1450 his printing experiments had apparently reached a considerable degree of refinement, for he was able to

Gutenberg's printing press revolutionized the way people spread information and shared knowledge.

persuade Johann Fust, a wealthy financier, to lend him 800 guilders—a very substantial capital investment, for which the tools and equipment for printing were to act as securities. Two years later Fust made an investment of an additional 800 guilders for a partnership in the enterprise. Fust and Gutenberg eventually became estranged, Fust, apparently, wanting a safe and quick return on his investment, while Gutenberg aimed at perfection rather than promptness.

Fust won a suit against him, the record of which is preserved, in part, in what is called the *Helmaspergersches Notariatsinstrument* ("the Helmasperger notarial instrument"), dated November 6, 1455, now in the library of the University of Göttingen. Gutenberg was ordered to pay Fust the total sum of the two loans and compound interest (probably totaling 2,020 guilders). Traditional historiography suggested that this settlement ruined Gutenberg, but more recent scholarship suggests that it favored him, allowing him to operate a printing shop through the 1450s and maybe into the 1460s.

Printing of the Bible

There is no reason to doubt that the printing of certain books (*werck der bucher*, specifically mentioned in the record of the trial, refers to the Forty-two-Line Bible that was Gutenberg's masterpiece) was completed, according to Gutenberg's major biographers, in 1455 at the latest. It has been estimated that the sale of the Forty-two-Line Bible alone would have produced many times over the sum owed Fust by Gutenberg, and there exists no explanation as to why these tangible assets were not counted among Gutenberg's property at the trial.

After winning his suit, Fust gained control of the type for the Bible and for Gutenberg's second masterpiece, a

Psalter, and at least some of Gutenberg's other printing equipment. He continued to print, using Gutenberg's materials, with the assistance of Peter Schöffer, his son-in-law, who had been Gutenberg's most skilled employee and a witness against him in the 1455 trial. The first printed book in Europe to bear the name of its printer is a magnificent Psalter completed in Mainz on August 14, 1457, which lists Johann Fust and Peter Schöffer.

The Psalter is decorated with hundreds of two-color initial letters and delicate scroll borders that were printed using a most ingenious technique based on multiple inking on a single metal block. Most experts are agreed that it would have been impossible for Fust and Schöffer alone to have invented and executed the intricate technical equipment necessary to executed this process between November 6, 1455, when Gutenberg lost control of his printing establishment, and August 14, 1457, when the Psalter appeared. It was Gutenberg's genius that was responsible for the Psalter decorations. In the 1960s it was suggested that he may also have had a hand in the creation of copper engraving, in which he may have recognized a method for producing pictorial matrices from which to cast reliefs that could be set with the type, initial letters, and calligraphic scrolls. It is at present no more than a hypothesis, but Gutenberg's absorption in both copper engraving and the Psalter decorations would certainly have increased Johann Fust's impatience and vindictiveness.

A number of other printings used to be attributed to Gutenberg. They are now considered the work of other minor printers; among these is a Thirty-six-Line Bible printed in Bamberg, a typographic resetting of the Forty-two-Line Bible. Attributed to Gutenberg himself is a *Türkenkalender*, a warning against the impending danger of Turkish invasion after the fall of Constantinople in

1453, printed December 1454 for 1455 use, some letters of indulgence, and some school grammars. The identity of the printer of a *Missale Speciale Constantiense* is still not established, but it was probably produced about 1473 in Basel, Switzerland.

In January 1465 the archbishop of Mainz pensioned Gutenberg, giving him an annual measure of grain, wine, and clothing and exempting him from certain taxes. His financial status in his last years has been debated but was probably not destitute.

CHRISTIAAN HUYGENS

(b. April 14, 1629, The Hague, Neth.—d. July 8, 1695, The Hague)

Christiaan Huygens (or Christian Huyghens) was a Dutch mathematician, astronomer, and physicist who founded the wave theory of light, discovered the true shape of the rings of Saturn, and made original contributions to the science of dynamics—the study of the action of forces on bodies. He was responsible for the practical application of the pendulum as a time controller in clocks.

Huygens was from a wealthy and distinguished middle-class family. His father, Constantijn Huygens, a diplomat, Latinist, and poet, was the friend and correspondent of many outstanding intellectual figures of the day, including the scientist and philosopher René Descartes. From an early age, Huygens showed a marked mechanical bent and a talent for drawing and mathematics. Some of his early efforts in geometry impressed Descartes, who was an occasional visitor to the Huygens's household. In 1645 Huygens entered the University of Leiden, where he studied mathematics and law. Two years later he entered the College of Breda, in the midst of a furious controversy over the philosophy of Descartes. Although Huygens later rejected certain of the Cartesian

As an inventor, Christiaan Huygens is well-known for his pendulum clock and telescope designs.

tenets including the identification of extension and body, he always affirmed that mechanical explanations were essential in science, a fact that later was to have an important influence on his mathematical interpretation of both light and gravitation.

In 1655 Huygens for the first time visited Paris, where his distinguished parentage, wealth, and affable disposition gave him entry to the highest intellectual and social circles. During his next visit to Paris in 1660, he met Blaise Pascal, with whom he had already been in correspondence on mathematical problems. Huygens had already acquired a European reputation by his publications in mathematics, especially his *De Circuli Magnitudine Inventa* of 1654, and by his discovery in 1659 of the true shape of the rings of Saturn—made possible by the improvements he had introduced in the construction of the telescope with his new method of grinding and polishing lenses. Using his improved telescope, he discovered a satellite of Saturn in March 1655 and distinguished the stellar components of the Orion nebula in 1656. His interest, as an astronomer, in the accurate measurement of time then led him to his discovery of the pendulum as a regulator of clocks, as described in his *Horologium* (1658).

In 1666 Huygens became one of the founding members of the French Academy of Sciences, which granted him a pension larger than that of any other member and an apartment in its building. Apart from occasional visits to Holland, he lived from 1666 to 1681 in Paris, where he made the acquaintance of the German mathematician and philosopher Gottfried Wilhelm Leibniz, with whom he remained on friendly terms for the rest of his life. The major event of Huygens's years in Paris was the publication in 1673 of his *Horologium Oscillatorium*. That brilliant work contained a theory on the mathematics of curvatures, as well as complete solutions to such problems of dynamics as the derivation of the formula for the time of oscillation of the simple pendulum, the oscillation of a body about a stationary axis, and the laws of centrifugal force for uniform circular motion. Some of the results were given without proof in an appendix, and Huygens's complete proofs were not published until after his death.

The treatment of rotating bodies was partly based on an ingenious application of the principle that in any system of bodies the center of gravity could never rise of its own accord above its initial position. Earlier Huygens had applied the same principle to the treatment of the problem of collisions, for which he had obtained a definitive solution in the case of perfectly elastic bodies as early as 1656, although his results remained unpublished until 1669.

The somewhat eulogistic dedication of the *Horologium Oscillatorium* to Louis XIV brought to a head murmurs against Huygens at a time when France was at war with Holland, but in spite of this he continued to reside in Paris. Huygens's health was never good, and he suffered from recurrent illnesses, including one in 1670 which was so serious that for a time he despaired of his own life.

A serious illness in 1681 prompted him to return to Holland, where he intended to stay only temporarily. But the death in 1683 of his patron, Jean-Baptiste Colbert, who had been Louis XIV's chief adviser, and Louis's increasingly reactionary policy, which culminated in the revocation (1685) of the Edict of Nantes, which had granted certain liberties to Protestants, militated against his ever returning to Paris.

Huygens visited London in 1689 and met Sir Isaac Newton and lectured on his own theory of gravitation before the Royal Society. Although he did not engage in public controversy with Newton directly, it is evident from Huygens's correspondence, especially that with Leibniz, that in spite of his generous admiration for the mathematical ingenuity of the *Principia*, he regarded a theory of gravity that was devoid of any mechanical explanation as fundamentally unacceptable. His own theory, published in 1690 in his *Discours de la cause de la pesanteur* ("Discourse on the Cause of Gravity"), though dating at least to 1669, included a mechanical explanation of gravity based on Cartesian vortices. Huygens's *Traité de la Lumière* (*Treatise on Light*), already largely completed by 1678, was also published in 1690. In it he again showed his need for ultimate mechanical explanations in his discussion of the nature of light. But his beautiful explanations of reflection and refraction—far superior to those of Newton—were entirely independent of mechanical explanations, being based solely on the so-called Huygens's principle of secondary wave fronts.

As a mathematician Huygens had great talent rather than genius of the first order. He sometimes found difficulty in following the innovations of Leibniz and others, but he was admired by Newton because of his love for the old synthetic methods. For almost the whole of the 18th century his work in both dynamics and light was overshadowed by that of Newton. In gravitation his theory was never taken seriously and remains today of historical interest only. But his work on rotating bodies and his contributions to the theory of light were of lasting importance. Forgotten until the early 19th century, these latter appear today as some of the most brilliant and original contributions to modern science and will always be remembered by the principle bearing his name.

The last five years of Huygens's life were marked by continued ill health and increasing feelings of loneliness and melancholy. He made the final corrections to his will in March 1695 and died after much suffering later that same year.

ANTONIE VAN LEEUWENHOEK

(b. Oct. 24, 1632, Delft, Neth.—d. Aug. 26, 1723, Delft)

Antonie van Leeuwenhoek was a Dutch microscopist who was the first to observe bacteria and protozoa. His researches on lower animals refuted the doctrine of spontaneous generation, and his observations helped lay the foundations for the sciences of bacteriology and protozoology.

Little is known of Leeuwenhoek's early life. When his stepfather died in 1648, he was sent to Amsterdam to become an apprentice to a linen draper. Returning to Delft when he was 20, he established himself as a draper and haberdasher. In 1660 he obtained a position as chamberlain to the sheriffs of Delft. His income was thus secure and sufficient enough to enable him to devote much of his time to his all-absorbing hobby, that of grinding lenses and using them to study tiny objects.

Leeuwenhoek made microscopes consisting of a single, high-quality lens of very short focal length; at the time, such simple microscopes were preferable to the compound microscope, which increased the problem of chromatic aberration. Although Leeuwenhoek's studies lacked the organization of formal scientific research, his powers of careful observation enabled him to make discoveries of fundamental importance. In 1674 he began to observe bacteria and protozoa, his "very little animalcules," which he was able to isolate from different sources, such as rainwater, pond and well water, and the human mouth and intestine, and he calculated their sizes.

In 1677 he described for the first time the spermatozoa from insects, dogs, and man, though Stephen Hamm probably was a codiscoverer. Leeuwenhoek studied the structure of the optic lens, striations in muscles, the

Antonie van Leeuwenhoek is considered to be the father of microscopy.

mouthparts of insects, and the fine structure of plants and discovered parthenogenesis in aphids. In 1680 he noticed that yeasts consist of minute globular particles. He extended Marcello Malpighi's demonstration in 1660 of the blood capillaries by giving (in 1684) the first accurate description of red blood cells. In his observations on rotifers in 1702, Leeuwenhoek remarked that "in all falling rain, carried from gutters into water-butts, animalcules are to be found; and that in all kinds of water, standing in the open air, animalcules can turn up. For these animalcules can be carried over by the wind, along with the bits of dust floating in the air."

A friend of Leeuwenhoek put him in touch with the Royal Society of England, to which, from 1673 until 1723, he communicated by means of informal letters most of his discoveries and to which he was elected a fellow in 1680. His discoveries were for the most part made public in the society's *Philosophical Transactions*. The first representation of bacteria is to be found in a drawing by Leeuwenhoek in that publication in 1683.

His researches on the life histories of various low forms of animal life were in opposition to the doctrine that they could be produced spontaneously or bred from corruption. Thus, he showed that the weevils of granaries (in his time commonly supposed to be bred from wheat as well as in it) are really grubs hatched from eggs deposited by winged insects. His letter on the flea, in which he not only described its structure but traced out the whole history of its metamorphosis, is of great interest, not so much for the exactness of his observations as for an illustration of his opposition to the spontaneous generation of many lower organisms, such as "this minute and despised creature." Some theorists asserted that the flea was produced from sand, others from dust or the like, but Leeuwenhoek proved that it bred in the regular way of winged insects.

Leeuwenhoek also carefully studied the history of the ant and was the first to show that what had been commonly reputed to be ants' eggs were really their pupae, containing the perfect insect nearly ready for emergence, and that the true eggs were much smaller and gave origin to maggots, or larvae. He argued that the sea mussel and other shellfish were not generated out of sand found at the seashore or mud in the beds of rivers at low water but from spawn, by the regular course of generation. He maintained the same to be true of the freshwater mussel, whose embryos he examined so carefully that he was able to observe how they were consumed by "animalcules," many of which, according to his description, must have included ciliates in conjugation, flagellates, and the *Vorticella*. Similarly, he investigated the generation of eels, which were at that time supposed to be produced from dew without the ordinary process of generation.

The dramatic nature of his discoveries made him world famous, and he was visited by many notables—including Peter I the Great of Russia, James II of England, and Frederick II the Great of Prussia.

Leeuwenhoek's methods of microscopy, which he kept secret, remain something of a mystery. During his lifetime he ground more than 400 lenses, most of which were very small—some no larger than a pinhead—and usually mounted them between two thin brass plates, riveted together. A large sample of these lenses, bequeathed to the Royal Society, were found to have magnifying powers of between 50 and, at the most, 300 times. In order to observe phenomena as small as bacteria, Leeuwenhoek must have employed some form of oblique illumination, or other technique, for enhancing the effectiveness of the lens, but this method he would not reveal. Leeuwenhoek continued his work almost to the end of his long life.

Leeuwenhoek's contributions to the *Philosophical Transactions* amounted to 375 and those to the *Memoirs of the Paris Academy of Sciences* to 27. Two collections of his works appeared during his life, one in Dutch (1685–1718) and the other in Latin (1715–22); a selection was translated by S. Hoole, *The Select Works of A. van Leeuwenhoek (1798–1807)*.

BENJAMIN FRANKLIN

(b. Jan. 17 [Jan. 6, Old Style], 1706, Boston, MA [now in U.S.]—d. April 17, 1790, Philadelphia, PA, U.S.)

Benjamin Franklin was an American printer and publisher, author, inventor and scientist, and diplomat. One of the foremost of the Founding Fathers, Franklin helped draft the Declaration of Independence and was one of its signers, represented the United States in France during the American Revolution, and was a delegate to the Constitutional Convention. He made important contributions to science, especially in the understanding of electricity, and is remembered for the wit, wisdom, and elegance of his writing.

Early Life

Ben Franklin was born the 10th son of the 17 children of a man who made soap and candles, one of the lowliest of the artisan crafts. In an age that privileged the firstborn son, Franklin was, as he tartly noted in his *Autobiography*, "the youngest Son of the youngest Son for five Generations back." He learned to read very early and had one year in grammar school and another under a private teacher, but his formal education ended at age 10. At 12 he was apprenticed to his brother James, a printer. His mastery of the printer's trade, of which he was proud to the end of his life, was achieved between 1718 and 1723. In the same period he read tirelessly and taught himself to write effectively.

His first enthusiasm was for poetry, but, discouraged with the quality of his own, he gave it up. Prose was another matter. Young Franklin discovered a volume of *The Spectator*—featuring Joseph Addison and Sir Richard Steele's famous periodical essays, which had appeared in England in 1711–12—and saw in it a means for improving his writing. He read these *Spectator* papers over and over, copied and recopied them, and then tried to recall them from memory. He even turned them into poetry and then back into prose. Franklin realized, as all the Founders did, that writing competently was such a rare talent in the 18th century that anyone who could do it well immediately attracted attention. "Prose writing" became, as he recalled in his *Autobiography*, "of great Use to me in the Course of my Life, and was a principal Means of my Advancement."

In 1721 James Franklin founded a weekly newspaper, the *New-England Courant*, to which readers were invited to contribute. Benjamin, now 16, read and perhaps set in type these contributions and decided that he could do as well himself. In 1722 he wrote a series of 14 essays signed "Silence Dogood" in which he lampooned everything from funeral eulogies to the students of Harvard College. For one so young to assume the persona of a middle-aged woman was a remarkable feat, and Franklin took "exquisite Pleasure" in the fact that his brother and others became convinced that only a learned and ingenious wit could have written these essays.

Late in 1722 James Franklin got into trouble with the provincial authorities and was forbidden to print or publish the *Courant*. To keep the paper going, he discharged his younger brother from his original apprenticeship and made him the paper's nominal publisher. New indentures were drawn up but not made public. Some months later, after a bitter quarrel, Benjamin secretly left home, sure that James would not "go to law" and reveal the subterfuge he had devised.

Youthful Adventures

Failing to find work in New York City, Franklin at age 17 went on to Quaker-dominated Philadelphia, a much more open and religiously tolerant place than Puritan Boston. One of the most memorable scenes of the *Autobiography* is the description of his arrival on a Sunday morning, tired and hungry. Finding a bakery, he asked for three pennies' worth of bread and got "three great Puffy Rolls." Carrying one under each arm and munching on the third, he walked up Market Street past the door of the Read family, where stood Deborah, his future wife. She saw him and "thought I made, as I certainly did, a most awkward ridiculous Appearance."

A few weeks later he was rooming at the Reads' and employed as a printer. By the spring of 1724 he was enjoying the companionship of other young men with a taste for reading, and he was also being urged to set up in business for himself by the governor of Pennsylvania, Sir William Keith. At Keith's suggestion, Franklin returned to Boston to try to raise the necessary capital. His father thought him too young for such a venture, so Keith offered to foot the bill himself and arranged Franklin's passage to England so that he could choose his type and make connections with London stationers and booksellers. Franklin exchanged "some promises" about marriage with Deborah Read and, with a young friend, James Ralph, as his companion, sailed for London in November 1724, just over a year after arriving in Philadelphia. Not until his ship was well out at sea did he realize that Governor Keith had not delivered the letters of credit and introduction he had promised.

In London Franklin quickly found employment in his trade and was able to lend money to Ralph, who was trying to establish himself as a writer. The two young men enjoyed the theater and the other pleasures of the city, including women. While in London, Franklin wrote *A Dissertation on Liberty and Necessity, Pleasure and Pain* (1725), a Deistical pamphlet inspired by his having set type for William Wollaston's moral tract, *The Religion of Nature Delineated.* Franklin argued in his essay that since human beings have no real freedom of choice, they are not morally responsible for their actions. This was perhaps a nice justification for his self-indulgent behavior in London and his ignoring of Deborah, to whom he had written only once. He later repudiated the pamphlet, burning all but one of the copies still in his possession.

By 1726 Franklin was tiring of London. He considered becoming an itinerant teacher of swimming, but, when Thomas Denham, a Quaker merchant, offered him a clerkship in his store in Philadelphia with a prospect of fat commissions in the West Indian trade, he decided to return home.

Achievement of Security and Fame

Denham died, however, a few months after Franklin entered his store. The young man, now 20, returned to the printing trade and in 1728 was able to set up a partnership with a friend. Two years later he borrowed money to become sole proprietor.

His private life at this time was extremely complicated. Deborah Read had married, but her husband had deserted her and disappeared. One matchmaking venture failed because Franklin wanted a dowry of £100 to pay off his business debt. A strong sexual drive, "that hard-to-be-govern'd Passion of Youth," was sending him to "low Women," and he thought he very much needed to get married. His affection for Deborah having "revived," he "took her to Wife" on September 1, 1730. At this point Deborah may have been the only woman in Philadelphia who would have him, for he brought to the marriage an illegitimate son, William, just borne of a woman who has never been identified. Franklin's common-law marriage lasted until Deborah's death in 1774. They had a son, Franky, who died at age four, and a daughter, Sarah, who survived them both. William was brought up in the household and apparently did not get along well with Deborah.

Franklin and his partner's first coup was securing the printing of Pennsylvania's paper currency. Franklin helped get this business by writing *A Modest Enquiry into the Nature and Necessity of a Paper Currency* (1729), and later he also became public printer of New Jersey, Delaware, and Maryland. Other moneymaking ventures included the *Pennsylvania Gazette*, published by Franklin from 1729 and generally acknowledged as among the best of the colonial newspapers, and *Poor Richard's Almanac*, printed annually from 1732 to 1757. Despite some failures, Franklin prospered. Indeed, he made enough to lend money with interest and to invest in rental properties in Philadelphia and many coastal towns. He had franchises or partnerships with printers in the Carolinas, New York, and the British West Indies. By the late 1740s he had become one of the wealthiest colonists in the northern part of the North American continent.

As he made money, he concocted a variety of projects for social improvement. In 1727 he organized the Junto, or Leather Apron Club, to debate questions of morals, politics, and natural philosophy and to exchange knowledge of business affairs. The need of Junto members for easier access to books led in 1731 to the organization of the Library Company of Philadelphia. Through the Junto, Franklin proposed a paid city watch, or police force. A paper read to the same group resulted in the organization of a volunteer fire company. In 1743 he sought an intercolonial version of the Junto, which led to the formation of the American Philosophical Society. In 1749 he published *Proposals Relating to the Education of Youth in Pennsilvania*; in 1751 the Academy of Philadelphia, from which grew the University of Pennsylvania, was founded. He also became an enthusiastic member of the Freemasons and promoted their "enlightened" causes.

Although still a tradesman, he was picking up some political offices. He became clerk of the Pennsylvania legislature in 1736 and postmaster of Philadelphia in 1737. Prior to 1748, though, his most important political service was his part in organizing a militia for the defense of the colony against possible invasion by the French and the Spaniards, whose privateers were operating in the Delaware River.

In 1748 Franklin, at age 42, had become wealthy enough to retire from active business. He took off his leather apron and became a gentleman, a distinctive status in the 18th century. Since no busy artisan could be a gentleman, Franklin never again worked as a printer; instead, he became a silent partner in the printing firm of Franklin and Hall, realizing in the next 18 years an average profit of over £600 annually. He announced his new status as a gentleman by having his portrait painted in a velvet coat and a brown wig; he also acquired a coat of arms, bought several slaves, and moved to a new and more spacious house in "a more quiet Part of the Town." Most important, as a gentleman and "master of [his] own time," he decided

The lightening rod, bifocals, and the Franklin stove are some of Benjamin Franklin's most famous inventions.

to do what other gentlemen did—engage in what he termed "Philosophical Studies and Amusements."

Scientific Studies

In the 1740s electricity was one of these curious amusements. It was introduced to Philadelphians by an electrical machine sent to the Library Company by one of Franklin's English correspondents. In the winter of 1746–47, Franklin and three of his friends began to investigate electrical phenomena. Franklin sent piecemeal reports of his ideas and experiments to Peter Collinson, his Quaker correspondent in London. Since he did not know what European scientists might have already discovered, Franklin set forth his findings timidly. In 1751 Collinson had Franklin's papers published in an 86-page book titled *Experiments and Observations on Electricity*. In the 18th century the book went through five English editions, three in French, and one each in Italian and German.

Franklin's fame spread rapidly. The experiment he suggested to prove the identity of lightning and electricity was apparently first made in France before he tried the simpler but more dangerous expedient of flying a kite in a thunderstorm. But his other findings were original. He created the distinction between insulators and conductors. He invented a battery for storing electrical charges. He coined new English words for the new science of electricity—*conductor*, *charge*, *discharge*, *condense*, *armature*, *electrify*, and others. He showed that electricity was a single "fluid" with positive and negative or plus and minus charges and not, as traditionally thought, two kinds of fluids. And he demonstrated that the plus and minus charges, or states of electrification of bodies, had to occur in exactly equal amounts—a crucial scientific principle known today as the law of conservation of charge.

Public Service in Later Life

Franklin was not only the most famous American in the 18th century but also one of the most famous figures in the Western world of the 18th century; indeed, he is one of the most celebrated and influential Americans who has ever lived. Although one is apt to think of Franklin exclusively as an inventor, as an early version of Thomas Edison, which he was, his 18th-century fame came not simply from his many inventions but, more important, from his fundamental contributions to the science of electricity. If there had been a Nobel Prize for Physics in the 18th century, Franklin would have been a contender. Enhancing his fame was the fact that he was an American, a simple man from an obscure background who emerged from the wilds of America to dazzle the entire intellectual world. Most Europeans in the 18th century thought of America as a primitive, undeveloped place full of forests and savages and scarcely capable of producing enlightened thinkers. Yet Franklin's electrical discoveries in the mid-18th century had surpassed the achievements of the most sophisticated scientists of Europe. Franklin became a living example of the natural untutored genius of the New World that was free from the encumbrances of a decadent and tired Old World—an image that he later parlayed into French support for the American Revolution.

Despite his great scientific achievements, however, Franklin always believed that public service was more important than science, and his political contributions to the formation of the United States were substantial. He had a hand in the writing of the Declaration of Independence, contributed to the drafting of the Articles of Confederation—America's first national constitution—and was the oldest member of the Constitutional Convention of 1787 that wrote the

Constitution of the United States of America in Philadelphia. More important, as diplomatic representative of the new American republic in France during the Revolution, he secured both diplomatic recognition and financial and military aid from the government of Louis XVI and was a crucial member of the commission that negotiated the treaty by which Great Britain recognized its former 13 colonies as a sovereign nation. Since no one else could have accomplished all that he did in France during the Revolution, he can quite plausibly be regarded as America's greatest diplomat.

Equally significant perhaps were Franklin's many contributions to the comfort and safety of daily life, especially in his adopted city of Philadelphia. No civic project was too large or too small for his interest. In addition to his lightning rod and his Franklin stove (a wood-burning stove that warmed American homes for more than 200 years), he invented bifocal glasses, the odometer, and the glass harmonica (armonica). He had ideas about everything—from the nature of the Gulf Stream to the cause of the common cold. He suggested the notions of matching grants and Daylight Saving Time. Almost single-handedly he helped to create a civic society for the inhabitants of Philadelphia. Moreover, he helped to establish new institutions that people now take for granted: a fire company, a library, an insurance company, an academy, and a hospital.

Probably Franklin's most important invention was himself. He created so many personas in his newspaper writings and almanac and in his posthumously published *Autobiography* that it is difficult to know who he really was. Following his death in 1790, he became so identified during the 19th century with the persona of his *Autobiography* and the Poor Richard maxims of his almanac—e.g., "Early to bed, early to rise, makes a man healthy, wealthy, and wise"—that he acquired the image of the self-made moralist obsessed with the getting and saving of money. Consequently, many imaginative writers, such as Edgar Allan Poe, Henry David Thoreau, Herman Melville, Mark Twain, and D.H. Lawrence, attacked Franklin as a symbol of America's middle-class moneymaking business values. Indeed, early in the 20th century the famous German sociologist Max Weber found Franklin to be the perfect exemplar of the "Protestant ethic" and the modern capitalistic spirit. Although Franklin did indeed become a wealthy tradesman by his early 40s, when he retired from his business, during his lifetime in the 18th century he was not identified as a self-made businessman or a budding capitalist. That image was a creation of the 19th century. But as long as America continues to be pictured as the land of enterprise and opportunity, where striving and hard work can lead to success, then that image of Franklin is the one that is likely to endure.

JAMES WATT

(b. Jan. 19, 1736, Greenock, Renfrewshire, Scot.—d. Aug. 25, 1819, Heathfield Hall, near Birmingham, Warwick, Eng.)

James Watt was a Scottish instrument maker and inventor whose steam engine contributed substantially to the Industrial Revolution. He was elected fellow of the Royal Society of London in 1785.

Education and Training

Watt's father, the treasurer and magistrate of Greenock, ran a successful ship- and house-building business. A delicate child, Watt was taught for a time at home by his mother; later, in grammar school, he learned Latin, Greek, and mathematics. The source for an important part of his education was his father's workshops, where, with his own tools, bench, and forge, he made models (e.g., of cranes and barrel organs) and grew familiar with ships' instruments.

Deciding at age 17 to be a mathematical-instrument maker, Watt first went to Glasgow, where one of his mother's relatives taught at the university, then, in 1755, to London, where he found a master to train him. Although his health broke down within a year, he had learned enough in that time "to work as well as most journeymen." Returning to Glasgow, he opened a shop in 1757 at the university and made mathematical instruments (e.g., quadrants, compasses, scales). He met many scientists and became a friend of Joseph Black, who developed the concept of latent heat. In 1764 he married his cousin Margaret Miller, who, before she died nine years later, bore him six children.

The Watt Engine

While repairing a model Newcomen steam engine in 1764 Watt was impressed by its waste of steam. In May 1765, after wrestling with the problem of improving it, he suddenly came upon a solution—the separate condenser, his first and greatest invention. Watt had realized that the loss of latent heat (the heat involved in changing the state of a substance—e.g., solid or liquid) was the worst defect of the Newcomen engine and that therefore condensation must be effected in a chamber distinct from the cylinder but connected to it. Shortly afterward, he met John Roebuck, the founder of the Carron Works, who urged him to make an engine. He entered into partnership with him in 1768, after having made a small test engine with the help of loans from Joseph Black. The following year Watt

James Watt's steam engine helped propel the Industrial Revolution.

took out the famous patent for "A New Invented Method of Lessening the Consumption of Steam and Fuel in Fire Engines."

Meanwhile, Watt in 1766 became a land surveyor; for the next eight years he was continuously busy marking out routes for canals in Scotland, work that prevented his making further progress with the steam engine. After Roebuck went bankrupt in 1772, Matthew Boulton, the manufacturer of the Soho Works in Birmingham, took over a share in Watt's patent. Bored with surveying and with Scotland, Watt immigrated to Birmingham in 1774.

After Watt's patent was extended by an act of Parliament, he and Boulton in 1775 began a partnership that lasted 25 years. Boulton's financial support made possible rapid progress with the engine. In 1776 two engines were installed, one for pumping water in a Staffordshire colliery, the other for blowing air into the furnaces of John Wilkinson, the famous ironmaster. That year Watt married again—his second wife, Ann MacGregor, bore him two more children.

During the next five years, until 1781, Watt spent long periods in Cornwall, where he installed and supervised numerous pumping engines for the copper and tin mines, the managers of which wanted to reduce fuel costs. Watt, who was no businessman, was obliged to endure keen bargaining in order to obtain adequate royalties on the new engines. By 1780 he was doing well financially, though Boulton still had problems raising capital. In the following year Boulton, foreseeing a new market in the corn, malt, and cotton mills, urged Watt to invent a rotary motion for the steam engine, to replace the reciprocating action of the original. He did this in 1781 with his so-called sun-and-planet gear, by means of which a shaft produced two revolutions for each cycle of the engine. In 1782, at the height of his inventive powers, he patented the double-acting engine, in which the piston pushed as well as pulled. The engine required a new method of rigidly connecting the piston to the beam. He solved this problem in 1784 with his invention of the parallel motion—an arrangement of connected rods that guided the piston rod in a perpendicular motion—which he described as "one of the most ingenious, simple pieces of mechanism I have contrived." Four years later his application of the centrifugal governor for automatic control of the speed of the engine, at Boulton's suggestion, and in 1790 his invention of a pressure gauge, virtually completed the Watt engine.

Later Years

Demands for his engine came quickly from paper mills, flour mills, cotton mills, iron mills, distilleries, and canals and waterworks. By 1790 Watt was a wealthy man, having received £76,000 in royalties on his patents in 11 years. The steam engine did not absorb all his attention, however. He was a member of the Lunar Society in Birmingham, a group of writers and scientists who wished to advance the sciences and the arts. Watt experimented on the strength of materials, and he was often involved in legal proceedings to protect his patents. In 1785 he and Boulton were elected fellows of the Royal Society of London. Watt then began to take holidays, bought an estate at Doldowlod, Radnorshire, and from 1795 onward gradually withdrew from business.

With the approach of his retirement in 1800 and because that was also the year in which his patents and partnership would expire, Watt established in 1794 the new firm of Boulton & Watt, which built the Soho Foundry to manufacture steam engines more competitively. During this time Watt's son by his first marriage, James, gave him anxiety. A youthful sympathizer with the French Revolution, he had been criticized in Parliament for presenting in 1792 an address from the Manchester Constitutional Society to the Société des Amis de la Constitution in Paris. After being cleared of political suspicion on his return home two years later, however, he and Boulton's son, Matthew, took over the management of the new firm.

Watt's long retirement was saddened by the deaths of a son by his second marriage, Gregory, and of many of his close friends. Nevertheless, he traveled with his wife to Scotland and to France and Germany when the Peace of Amiens was signed in 1802 and continued to work in the garret of his house, which he had equipped as a workshop. There he invented a sculpturing machine with which he reproduced original busts and figures for his friends. He also acted as consultant to the Glasgow Water Company. His achievements were amply recognized in his lifetime: he was made doctor of laws of the University of Glasgow in 1806 and a foreign associate of the French Academy of Sciences in 1814 and was offered a baronetcy, which he declined.

JOSEPH AND ÉTIENNE MONTGOLFIER

respectively, (b. Aug. 26, 1740, Annonay, France—d. June 26, 1810, Balaruc-les-Bains); (b. Jan. 6, 1745, Annonay, France—d. Aug. 2, 1799, enroute from Lyon to Annonay)

The Montgolfier brothers, Joseph-Michel and Jacques-Étienne, were French pioneer developers of the hot-air balloon who conducted the first untethered flights. Modifications and improvements of the basic Montgolfier design were incorporated in the construction of larger balloons that, in later years, opened the way to exploration of the upper atmosphere.

Joseph and Étienne were 2 of the 16 children of Pierre Montgolfier, whose prosperous paper factories in the small town of Vidalon, near Annonay, in southern France, ensured the financial support of their balloon experiments. While carrying on their father's paper business, they maintained their interest in scientific experimentation.

In 1782 they discovered that heated air, when collected inside a large lightweight paper or fabric bag, caused the bag to rise into the air. (According to one, possibly apocryphal, story, the brothers took inspiration from watching Joseph's wife's skirts as they billowed in the kitchen from the heat of a charcoal burner being used to dry laundry.) The Montgolfiers made the first public demonstration of their discovery on June 4, 1783, at the marketplace in Annonay. They filled their 35-foot- (10.5 m) diameter balloon with heated air by burning straw and wool under the opening at the bottom of the bag. The balloon rose into the air about 3,000 feet (1,000 m), remained there some 10 minutes, and then settled to the ground more than a mile and a half from where it rose. The Montgolfiers traveled to Paris and then to Versailles, where they repeated the experiment with a larger balloon on September 19, 1783, sending a sheep, a rooster, and a duck aloft as passengers. The balloon floated for about 8 minutes and landed safely about 2 miles (3.2 km) from the launch site. On November 21, 1783, the first manned untethered flight took place in a Montgolfier balloon with Pilatre de Rozier and François Laurent, marquis d'Arlandes, as passengers. The balloon sailed over Paris for 5.5 miles (9 kilometers) in about 25 minutes.

The two brothers were honored by the French Académie des Sciences. They published books on aeronautics and continued their scientific careers. Joseph invented a calorimeter and the hydraulic ram, and Étienne developed a process for manufacturing vellum.

ALESSANDRO VOLTA

(b. Feb. 18, 1745, Como, Lombardy [now in Italy]—d. March 5, 1827, Como)

Alessandro Giuseppe Antonio Anastasio Volta (also known as Count Volta) was an Italian physicist whose invention of the electric battery provided the first source of continuous current.

In 1775 Volta's interest in electricity led him to invent the electrophorus, a device used to generate static electricity. He became professor of physics at the Royal School of Como in 1774 and discovered and isolated methane gas in 1778. One year later he was appointed to the chair of physics at the University of Pavia.

In 1780 Volta's friend Luigi Galvani discovered that contact of two different metals with the muscle of a frog resulted in the generation of an electric current. Volta had been studying how electricity stimulates the senses of touch, taste, and sight. When Volta put a metal coin on top of his tongue and another coin of a different metal under his tongue and connected their surfaces with a wire, the coins tasted salty. Like Galvani, Volta assumed that he was working with animal electricity until 1796 when he discovered that he could also produce a current when he substituted a piece of cardboard soaked in brine for his tongue. Volta correctly conjectured that the effect was caused by the contact between metal and a moist body. Around 1800 he constructed what is now known as a voltaic pile consisting of layers of silver, moist cardboard, and zinc, repeated in that order, beginning and ending with a different metal. When he joined the silver and the zinc with a wire, electricity flowed continuously through the wire. This rudimentary form of battery produced a smaller voltage than the Leyden jar, an earlier device for storing static electricity, but it was easier to use because it could supply a steady current and did not have to be recharged.

In 1801 in Paris, Volta gave a demonstration of his battery's generation of electric current before Napoleon, who made Volta a count and senator of the kingdom of Lombardy. The emperor of Austria made him director of the philosophical faculty at the University of Padua in 1815. The volt, a unit of the electromotive force that drives current, was named in his honor in 1881.

JOSEPH-MARIE JACQUARD

(b. July 7, 1752, Lyon, France—d. Aug. 7, 1834, Oullins)

Joseph-Marie Jacquard was the French inventor of an automatic loom that served as the impetus for the technological revolution of the textile industry. The Jacquard loom also demonstrated the concept of a programmable machine; for this reason it is frequently considered to be a precursor of the digital computer.

Jacquard first formed the idea for his loom in 1790, but his work was cut short by the French Revolution, in which he fought on the side of the Revolutionaries in the defense of Lyon. In 1801 Jacquard demonstrated an improved drawloom, for which he was awarded a bronze medal. He continued his work, and in 1804–05 he introduced an attachment that has caused any loom that uses it to be called a Jacquard loom. The loom worked by tugging various-colored threads into patterns by means of an array of rods. By inserting a card punched with holes, an operator could control the motion of the rods and thereby alter the pattern of the weave. Moreover, the loom was equipped with a card-reading device that slipped a new card from a prepunched deck into place every time the shuttle was thrown, so that complex weaving patterns could be automated. In 1806 the loom was declared public property, and Jacquard was rewarded with a pension and a royalty on each machine.

His machine aroused bitter hostility among the silk weavers, who feared that its labor-saving capabilities would deprive them of jobs. The weavers of Lyon not only burned machines that were put into production but attacked Jacquard as well. Eventually, the advantages of the loom brought about its general acceptance, and by 1812 there were 11,000 in use in France. In 1819 Jacquard was awarded a gold medal and the Cross of the Legion of Honor. The use of his loom spread to England in the 1820s and from there virtually worldwide.

The Jacquard loom was a marvel of the Industrial Revolution. A textile-weaving loom, it could also be called the first practical information-processing device. What was extraordinary about the device was that it transferred the design process from a labor-intensive weaving stage to a card-punching stage. Once the cards had been punched and assembled, the design was complete, and the loom implemented the design automatically. The Jacquard loom, therefore, could be said to be programmed for different patterns by these decks of punched cards.

For those intent on mechanizing calculations, the Jacquard loom provided important lessons: the sequence of operations that a machine performs could be controlled to make the machine do something quite different; a punched card could be used as a medium for directing the machine; and, most important, a device could be directed to perform different tasks by feeding it instructions in a sort of language—i.e., making the machine programmable. It is not too great a stretch to say that, in the Jacquard loom, programming was invented before the computer. The punched cards were adopted by the noted English inventor Charles Babbage as an input-output medium for his proposed Analytical Engine, which is generally considered to be the first computer.

JOHN LOUDON McADAM

(b. Sept. 21, 1756, Ayr, Ayrshire, Scot.—d. Nov. 26, 1836, Moffat, Dumfriesshire)

John Loudon McAdam was a Scottish inventor of the macadam road surface.

In 1770 he went to New York City, entering the countinghouse of a merchant uncle; he returned to Scotland with a considerable fortune in 1783. There he purchased an estate at Sauhrie, Ayrshire. McAdam, who had become a road trustee in his district, noted that the local highways were in poor condition. At his own expense he undertook a series of experiments in road making.

In 1798 he moved to Falmouth, Cornwall, where he continued his experiments under a government appointment. In 1815, having been appointed surveyor general of the Bristol roads, he put his theories into practice. McAdam had no use for the masonry constructions of his predecessors and contemporaries. Instead, he showed that traffic could be supported by a relatively thin layer of small, single-sized, angular pieces of broken stone placed and compacted on a well-drained natural formation and covered by an impermeable surface of smaller stones. Drainage was essential to the success of McAdam's method, and he required the pavement to be elevated above the surrounding surface. The structural layer of broken stone was 8 inches (20.32 cm) thick and used stone of 2 to 3 inches

(5 to 8 cm) maximum size laid in layers and compacted by traffic—a process adequate for the traffic of the time. The top layer was 2 inches (5 cm) thick, using three-fourths- to 1-inch (2.5 cm) stone to fill surface voids between the large stones. Continuing maintenance was essential.

Although McAdam drew on the successes and failures of others, his total structural reliance on broken stone represented the largest paradigm shift in the history of road pavements. To document his work, McAdam wrote *Remarks on the Present System of Road-Making* (1816) and *Practical Essay on the Scientific Repair and Preservation of Roads* (1819).

As the result of a parliamentary inquiry in 1823 into the whole question of road making, McAdam's views were adopted by the public authorities, and in 1827 he was appointed Surveyor General of Metropolitan Roads in Great Britain. Macadamization of roads did much to facilitate travel and communication. The principles were quickly adopted in other countries, notably the United States, and are still used today.

NICÉPHORE NIÉPCE

(b. March 7, 1765, Chalon-sur-Saône, France—d. July 5, 1833, Chalon-sur-Saône)

Nicéphore Niépce was a French inventor who was the first to make a permanent photographic image.

The son of a wealthy family suspected of royalist sympathies, Niépce fled the French Revolution but returned to serve in the French army under Napoleon Bonaparte. Dismissed because of ill health, he settled near his native town of Chalon-sur-Saône, where he remained engaged in research for the rest of his life.

In 1807 Niépce and his brother Claude invented an

internal-combustion engine, which they called the Pyréolophore, explaining that the word was derived from a combination of the Greek words for "fire," "wind," and "I produce." Working on a piston-and-cylinder system similar to 20th-century gasoline-powered engines, the Pyréolophore initially used lycopodium powder for fuel, and Niépce claimed to have used it to power a boat.

When lithography became a fashionable hobby in France in 1813, Niépce began to experiment with the then-novel printing technique. Unskilled in drawing, and unable to obtain proper lithographic stone locally, he sought a way to provide images automatically. He coated pewter with various light-sensitive substances in an effort to copy superimposed engravings in sunlight. From this he progressed in April 1816 to attempts at photography, which he called heliography (sundrawing), with a camera. He recorded a view from his workroom window on paper sensitized with silver chloride but was only partially able to fix the image. Next he tried various types of supports for the light-sensitive material bitumen of Judea, a kind of asphalt, which hardens on exposure to light. Using this material he succeeded in 1822 in obtaining a photographic copy of an engraving superimposed on glass. In 1826/27, using a camera, he made a view from his workroom on a pewter plate, this being the first permanently fixed image from nature. Metal had the advantage of being unbreakable and was better suited to the subsequent etching process to produce a printing plate, which was Niépce's final aim. In 1826, he had produced another heliograph, a reproduction of an engraved portrait, which was etched by the Parisian engraver Augustin-François Lemaître, who pulled two prints. Thus Niépce not only solved the problem of reproducing nature by light, but he invented the first photomechanical reproduction process. While on a visit to England in 1827, Niépce addressed a memorandum on his invention to the Royal Society, London, but his insistence on keeping the method secret prevented the matter from being investigated.

Unable to reduce the very long exposure times by either chemical or optical means, Niépce in 1829 finally gave in to the repeated overtures of Louis-Jacques-Mandé Daguerre, a Parisian painter, for a partnership to perfect and exploit heliography. Niépce died without seeing any further advance, but, building on his knowledge, and working with his materials, Daguerre eventually succeeded in greatly reducing the exposure time through his discovery of a chemical process for development of (making visible) the latent (invisible) image formed upon brief exposure.

ROBERT FULTON

(b. Nov. 14, 1765, Lancaster county, PA [now in U.S.]—d. Feb. 24, 1815, New York, NY)

Robert Fulton was an American inventor, engineer, and artist who brought steamboating from the experimental stage to commercial success. He also designed a system of inland waterways, a submarine, and a steam warship.

Fulton was the son of Irish immigrants. When their unproductive farm was lost by mortgage foreclosure in 1771, the family moved to Lancaster, where Fulton's father died in 1774 (not 1786 as is generally written). Having learned to read and write at home, Fulton was sent at age eight to a Quaker school; later he became an apprentice in a Philadelphia jewelry shop, where he specialized in the painting of miniature portraits on ivory for lockets and rings.

After settling his mother on a small farm in western Pennsylvania in 1786, Fulton went to Bath, Virginia, to recover from a severe cough. There the paintings by the young man—tall, graceful, and an engaging conversationalist—were admired by people who advised him to study in Europe. On returning to Philadelphia, Fulton applied himself to painting and the search for a sponsor. Local merchants, eager to raise the city's cultural level, financed his passage to London in 1787.

Although Fulton's reception in London was cordial, his paintings made little impression; they showed neither the style nor the promise required to provide him more than a precarious living. Meanwhile, he became acquainted with new inventions for propelling boats: a water jet ejected by a steam pump and a single, mechanical paddle. His own experiments led him to conclude that several revolving paddles at the stern would be most effective.

Beginning in 1794, however, having admitted defeat as a painter, Fulton turned his principal efforts toward canal engineering. His *Treatise on the Improvement of Canal Navigation*, in 1796, dealt with a complete system of inland-water transportation based on small canals extending throughout the countryside. He included details on inclined planes for raising boats—he did not favor locks—aqueducts for valley crossings, boats for specialized cargo, and bridge designs featuring bowstring beams to transmit only vertical loads to the piers. A few bridges were built to his design in the British Isles, but his canal ideas were nowhere accepted.

Undaunted, he traveled in 1797 to Paris, where he proposed the idea of a submarine, the *Nautilus*, to be used in France's war with Britain; it would creep under the hulls of British warships and leave a powder charge to be exploded later. The French government rejected the idea, however, as an atrocious and dishonorable way to fight. In 1800 he was able to build the *Nautilus* at his own expense; he conducted trials on the Seine and finally obtained government sanction for an attack, but wind and tide enabled two British ships to elude his slow vessel.

In 1801 Fulton met Robert R. Livingston, a member of the committee that drafted the U.S. Declaration of Independence. Before becoming minister to France, Livingston had obtained a 20-year monopoly of steamboat navigation within the state of New York. The two men decided to share the expense of building a steamboat in Paris using Fulton's design—a side paddlewheel, 66-foot- (20 m) long boat, with an eight-horsepower engine of French design. Although the engine broke the hull, they were encouraged by success with another hull. Fulton ordered parts for a 24-horsepower engine from Boulton and Watt for a boat on the Hudson, and Livingston obtained an extension on his monopoly of steamboat navigation.

Returning to London in 1804, Fulton advanced his ideas with the British government for submersible and low-lying craft that would carry explosives in an attack. Two raids against the French using his novel craft, however, were unsuccessful. In 1805, after Nelson's victory at Trafalgar, it was apparent that Britain was in control of the seas without the aid of Fulton's temperamental weapons. In the same year, the parts for his projected steamboat were ready for shipment to the United States, but Fulton spent a desperate year attempting to collect money he felt the British owed him.

Maiden Voyage

Arriving in New York in December 1806, Fulton at once

set to work supervising the construction of the steamboat that had been planned in Paris with Livingston. He also attempted to interest the U.S. government in a submarine, but his demonstration of it was a fiasco. By early August 1807 a 150-foot- (45 m) long *Steamboat*, as Fulton called it, was ready for trials. Its single-cylinder condensing steam engine (24-inch bore and four-foot stroke) drove two 15-foot (4.6 m) diameter side paddlewheels; it consumed oak and pine fuel. The 150-mile (240 km) trial run from New York to Albany required 32 hours (an average of almost 4.7 miles [7.6 km] per hour), considerably better time than the 4 miles (6.4 km) per hour required by the monopoly. The passage was epic because sailing sloops required four days for the same trip.

After building an engine house, raising the bulwark, and installing berths in the cabins of the now-renamed *North River Steamboat*, Fulton began commercial trips in September. He made three round-trips fortnightly between New York and Albany, carrying passengers and light freight. Problems, however, remained: the mechanical difficulties, for example, and the jealous sloopboatmen, who through "inadvertence" would ram the unprotected paddlewheels of their new rivals. During the first winter season he stiffened and widened the hull, replaced the cast-iron crankshaft with a forging, fitted guards over the wheels, and improved passenger accommodations. These modifications made it a different boat, which was registered in 1808 as the *North River Steamboat of Clermont*, soon reduced to *Clermont* by the press.

In 1808 Fulton married his partner's niece, Harriet Livingston, by whom he had a son and three daughters.

In 1811 the Fulton-designed, Pittsburgh-built *New Orleans* was sent south to validate the Livingston–Fulton steamboat monopoly of the New Orleans Territory. The trip was slow and perilous, river conditions being desperate because of America's first recorded, and also largest, earthquake, which had destroyed New Madrid just below the confluence of the Ohio and Mississippi rivers. Fulton's low-powered vessel remained at New Orleans, for it could go no farther upstream than Natchez. He built three boats for Western rivers that were based at New Orleans, but none could conquer the passage to Pittsburgh.

Fulton was a member of the 1812 commission that recommended building the Erie Canal. With the English blockade the same year, he insisted that a mobile floating gun platform be built—the world's first steam warship—to protect New York Harbor against the British fleet. The *Demologos*, or *Fulton*, as the ship was alternately called, incorporated new and novel ideas: two parallel hulls, with paddlewheel between; the steam engine in one hull, and boilers and stacks in the other. It weighed 2,745 displacement tons and measured 156 feet (48 m) in length; a slow vessel, its speed did not exceed 6 knots (6 nautical miles, or 11 km, per hour). Launched in October 1814, the heavily gunned and armored steamship underwent successful sea trials but was never used in battle; when peace came in December, it was transferred to the Brooklyn Navy Yard, where it was destroyed by an accidental explosion in 1829.

By 1810 three of Fulton's boats served the Hudson and Raritan rivers. His steamboats also replaced the horse ferries that were used for heavily traveled river crossings in New York, Boston, and Philadelphia. He retained the typical broad double-ended hulls that needed no turning for the return passage. Manhattan's crosstown Fulton Street, named in 1816, was the principal thoroughfare connecting the two river terminals.

Fulton spent much of his wealth in litigations involving the pirating of patents relating to steamboats and in trying to suppress rival steamboat builders who found loopholes in the state-granted monopoly. His wealth was further depleted by his unsuccessful submarine projects, investments in paintings, and financial assistance to farmer kin and young artists. After testifying at a legal hearing in Trenton, early in 1815, he became chilled en route home to New York, where he died. His family made claims on the U.S. government for services rendered. A bill of $100,000 for the relief of the heirs finally passed the Congress in 1846 but was reduced to $76,300, with no interest.

A Hudson–Fulton Celebration in 1909 commemorated the success of the *North River Steamboat of Clermont* and the discovery in 1609 of the North River by the English navigator who was the first to sail upstream to Albany. A "Robert Fulton" commemorative stamp was issued in 1965, the bicentenary of his birth, and the two-story farmhouse, his birthplace, was acquired and restored by the Pennsylvania Historical and Museum Commission.

Glossary

archaeological: Relating to the study of past human life based on what those people left behind.

centrifugal force: A force that causes objects moving in a circle to move away from the center.

doctrine: A set of ideas or beliefs that are taught.

dynamics: The study of energy, motion, and force.

lithography: A printmaking method.

optics: The study of sight and light.

oscillation: The act of regularly moving from one position to another and back.

Paleolithic: Related to the earliest period of the Stone Age in which stone tools were used.

patent: Rights given to a person by the government to make, use, or sell an invention.

pendulum: A weighted stick that swings back and forth under the action of gravity.

primitive: Very simple and basic; not modern.

spontaneous generation: The false notion that organisms can spring to life from nonliving matter.

textile: A kind of cloth that's woven or knit.

For More Information

BOOKS

Alexander, Lori. *All in a Drop: How Antony van Leeuwenhoek Discovered an Invisible World.* New York, NY: Houghton Mifflin Harcourt, 2021.

Levy, Janey. *20 Fun Facts about the Steamboat.* Buffalo, NY: Gareth Stevens Publishing, 2024.

Lowe, Lindsey. *Discovering the Technology of Ancient Greece.* New York, NY: Cavendish Square Publishing, 2024.

Oachs, Emily Rose. *The Cave of Altamira.* Minneapolis, MN: Bellwether Media, Inc., 2020.

WEBSITES

The Franklin Institute
fi.edu/en/science-and-education/benjamin-franklin/inventions
Check out more of Benjamin Franklin's inventions, including swim fins!

Library of Congress
guides.loc.gov/gutenberg/the-printer
Learn about the life of Johannes Gutenberg and find out more about the copy of the Gutenberg Bible at the Library of Congress.

National Air and Space Museum
airandspace.si.edu/collection-objects/etienne-et-joseph-montgolfier/nasm_A19680079000
Read up on the Montgolfier brother and their experiments with flight.

Science and Industry Museum
www.scienceandindustrymuseum.org.uk/objects-and-stories/jacquard-loom
Find images and step-by-step descriptions of the Jacquard loom on this website, and learn how this invention revolutionized textile production.

Index